This book belongs to:

Creativity is the way I share my soul with the world.

# Tips and Tricks For Using This Coloring Book:

1. These charismatic Day of the Dead images have been conveniently placed on one side of the page to prevent bleeding.

2. Feel free to use markers, gel pens, colored pencils, or crayons. If you press down hard when you color, place a sheet of paper behind the page.

3. Light some candles, choose your favorite Latin American music and drink. Anti-stress as you relax, reflect, and rejuvenate as you color these delightful images.

4. Create your Day of the Dead festive setting, with these iconic images and interesting facts about the Day of The Dead sugar skulls, and tattoos.

5. Remember, this book has designed for adults and older children to learn, discuss, and color the iconic images of this annual festival.

Day of the Dead symbolic colors:
Black—death
Pink—celebration
Red—true love & passion
White—innocence and hope
Purple—grieving and suffering
Yellow & Orange—marigolds and the sun

I KNOW MY COLORS!
Before you start
coloring, make sure you
read the
interesting facts, and have
fun as you color!

The Day of the Dead celebration is called DIA DE LOS MUERTOS (Spanish) and is sometimes mistakenly associated with Halloween. However, they have nothing in common except for the skull design, costumes, and calendar dates.

The annual celebration of the Day of the Dead is a lovely time to remember family and friends. When you hang out with skeletons... you're reminded, you won't be around for a very long time!

THE DAY OF THE DEAD is a festival that begins on October 31st at midnight of All Hallow's Eve and continues until November 2nd, All Souls Day.

The celebration is a 3,500-year old ritual that honors departed loved ones, rulers, and warriors.

During the 16th century, the Spanish colonists took the local religion in Mexico and incorporated it with their rituals. The Day of the Dead is celebrated on November 1st and 2nd and remains one of the most significant celebrations in Mexico.

The Day of the Dead, now celebrated in Latin America, and many places throughout the world!

Families build altars, called Ofrendas (Spanish) in their homes to celebrate their lost loved ones.

Day Of Dead

The altars consist of many traditional elements: candles, sugar skulls, marigolds, water, food, and a favorite book or instrument of a loved.

Marigolds are the common flowers chosen for the festivals to attract the departed souls. They believe the path of the flower petals connect those who've passed to the surviving loved ones.

It's not a sad time, but a "fiesta" to remember and honor the deceased family & friends. Telling humorous stories about deceased family and friends is the best way to honor them.

On November 1st or 2nd, the celebration moves to the cemetery. First, graves and tombs are cleaned and decorated. Then music is played as family and friends eat, drink, sing, dance, and reminisce about their ancestors.

Red roses symbolize an undying passionate love.

Italian missionaries introduced the concept of sugar art in Mexico.

Sugar skulls, called Calaveras (Spanish), are brightly colored sugar skulls, usually made from sugar and sometimes ceramic.

Calaveras are not meant to be scary like Halloween decorations, they are happy, smiling, and colorful.

Sugar skulls come in many different sizes made of candy, decorated with icing, some add feathers, glitter, hats, flowers, and other objects to personalize them usually made out of candy.

The sugar skulls are meant to reflect the happy memories of past family and friends.

Sugar skulls are a reminder of the fragile boundary between life and death and the impulse to ritualize and revel in losses and love.

The Feria Del Alfenique Festival, a sugar skull design competition, is held annually in Mexico.

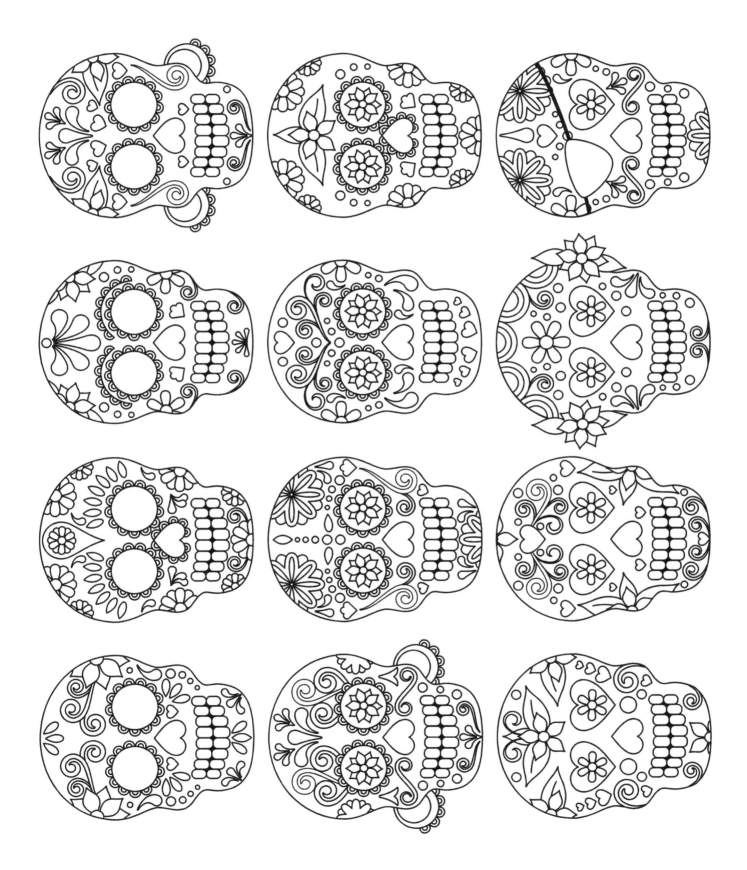

Face painting, tattoos, or wearing sugar skulls masks to celebrate the Day of the Dead has become very popular.

The Goddess Tattoo called "The Lady of the Dead" is one of the most iconic images for Day of the Dead tattoos.

Eye-catching tattoos!

Tattoos may symbolize present or past relationships.

Tattoos not only memorialize loved ones, but they also emphasize the belief in life after death.

Matching tattoos on partners show their committed love for each other. The best thing about Day of the Dead tattoos is that both men and women can wear them universally.

Tattoos with "Hope" and "Forever" express the fragility of human existence.

Day of the Dead tattoos can be both haunting and brilliant because many people don't understand their meanings. But those who do, love what they represent.

You will always be in my heart...
Because in there
You're still alive.

Those we love don't go away,
They walk beside us every day...
Unseen, unheard, but always near,
Still loved, still missed, and very dear!

Sometimes I still can't believe you're gone!

Florabella Publishing, LLC

I can no longer see you with my eyes
Touch you with my hands
I will feel you in my heart....Forever!

Thank you so much for your recent purchase.
We hope you're enjoying these delightful Day of
the Dead images, tattoos, and interesting facts.
Please visit our website for news about future
books and suggested friendly reads for children
and adults. Let us know if you'd like to see us
publish a book on another topic.

florabellapublishing.com
florabellapublishing@yahoo.com

IN THE END, IT'S NOT THE YEARS IN YOUR LIFE THAT
COUNT. IT'S THE LIFE IN YOUR YEARS.
Abraham Lincoln

Florabella Publishing, LLC